SAINT PHILIP HOWARD

Earl of Arundel

*F*ortune never shone with fairer promise than around the cradle of this highly favoured child and a bright future was predicted for him. He was heir to wide estates, great riches and many a noble name. His father, Thomas, 4th Duke of Norfolk, stood in high favour with Queen Mary and her consort, Philip of Spain, while his mother was heiress to the Earls of Arundel, the oldest earldom in the land.

A few days after his birth he was carried to the Chapel Royal at Whitehall and christened with much pomp and ceremony by the Archbishop of York, in the presence of the King and Queen and all their court. He was baptized in the special font of gold kept for the princes of the realm; his great grandmother, the old Duchess of Norfolk, was his godmother and held him in her arms, and he was given the name of Philip in honour of his godfather who was none other than the King himself.

Who could have foreseen that, in 38 years, the life begun amid such scenes of splendour would flicker slowly out in a lonely prison cell? And yet it is not for his short spell of earthly glory that the name of Philip, Earl of Arundel, is known but rather for the 11 long years of patient suffering in the Tower of London.

LIFE OF VEN. PHILIP HOWARD, *Cecil Kerr*

England in the Sixteenth Century

RIGHT:
The Arms of the Duke of Norfolk: these appear on the front of the shrine of St Philip in Arundel Cathedral.

The Tudor Dynasty had been firmly established when Henry VIII succeeded his father to the throne in 1509. Determined to secure the succession with a male heir, Henry married six times which led to the break from Rome of the English Church. His immediate heirs, the boy king, Edward VI, and Mary Tudor, both died within a few years of their accession and it was Elizabeth, the daughter of Henry's second marriage to Anne Boleyn, who was destined to rule for the remainder of the 16th century. During her reign the Protestant church was established on a firm basis in England; Catholics were persecuted by fines, imprisonment and, in the case of priests and those who helped them, execution.

Being not only a female but also an unmarried monarch, Elizabeth was inevitably the focus of intense domestic and international rivalry as ambitious nobles and princes vied for her hand in marriage and the control of her kingdom that would go with it; the question of the succession remained critical.

In the background Mary, Queen of Scots, whose grandmother was a daughter of Henry VII and a sister of Henry VIII, stood next in line to the throne should the children of Henry VIII fail to produce an heir. Mary was a Catholic and a focus of discontent against Queen Elizabeth and any foreign attempt to restore the

RIGHT:
Anne Boleyn, second wife of Henry VIII and mother of Elizabeth I. Both Anne and Catherine Howard (Henry VIII's fifth wife) were nieces of the 3rd Duke of Norfolk.

2

Catholic faith to England. When in 1568 Mary was forced to flee from Scotland she was held captive in England for 18 years – a period punctuated by plots to elevate her to the throne; for one of these Philip Howard's father was executed. Mary herself was beheaded in 1587. Elizabeth died without an heir in 1603 and, ironically, was succeeded by Mary's son, James I.

It was into this age of turmoil that Philip Howard was born as son and heir to the only duke in Tudor England.

LEFT:
Mary, Queen of Scots, next in line of succession should Elizabeth die without an heir. Philip's father was executed for his attempt to marry her and to put her on the throne.

LEFT:
Allegory of the Tudor succession showing Henry VIII with Mary Tudor and Philip of Spain (after whom Philip was named), Edward VI and Elizabeth I, all of whom were to be influential in Philip's life.

3

St Philip Howard's Family

RIGHT:

Mary Fitzalan, Philip's mother and first wife of the 4th Duke, who brought considerable estates into the family, including Arundel Castle.

RIGHT:

Arundel Castle, by James Canter (c.1770). The East Wing and the Keep are largely as Philip would have known them: the West Wing (to the left) was severely damaged during the Civil War.

Philip's father was Thomas Howard, 4th Duke of Norfolk. His mother was Lady Mary Fitzalan, daughter and heiress of Henry, 12th Earl of Arundel and Lord Steward of the Royal Household. The Duchess was only seventeen when Philip was born; she never rallied from her son's birth and died less than two months later on 25 August 1557.

The Duke soon married again. He had three children by his second wife, Margaret Audley, and after her death he married for a third time a widow, Elizabeth Dacre, who had a son and three daughters. By now the Duke was the richest man in England and, to keep his wealth in the family, his two sons, Philip and William, were betrothed to Anne and Bess Dacre.

Being in the forefront of public life, the Howard family had lived dangerously. The Duke's grandfather had only escaped the scaffold by the death of Henry VIII the night before he was due to be executed; and his father had been beheaded for including among his quarterings the royal arms (to which he was entitled) on the specious grounds that this indicated he had treasonable designs on the throne.

After the death of Elizabeth Dacre, the Duke attempted to marry Mary, Queen of Scots, but was thwarted by Queen Elizabeth. Subsequently he was arrested for his involvement in the Ridolphi Plot aimed at deposing Elizabeth and installing the Catholic Mary on the throne. He was committed to the Tower and beheaded on 2 June 1572; the Dukedom and the Howard estates were attainted (forfeited). Philip was then only fourteen but, through his mother, remained heir to the Earldom of Arundel and to the Fitzalan estates.

In 1564 the Duke had bought the site of the London Charterhouse, home of the Carthusian martyrs, and it was here that Philip was brought up. The Charterhouse, rebuilt as a splendid mansion called Howard House, was the place where, a number of years later, Philip's mass of reconciliation to the Catholic faith would be celebrated.

EARLY YEARS

LEFT:
Thomas Howard, Philip's father, 4th Duke of Norfolk and the only duke in Tudor England.

Philip's tutor was Gregory Martin, a brilliant fellow of St John's College, Oxford, who was later to become the principal translator of the Douai Bible. It was Gregory Martin who, from his self-imposed exile in Flanders, finally persuaded the young Edmund Campion to leave Oxford and declare himself a Catholic. Campion was later to have a decisive impact on Philip's future.

When he was fourteen, the age of full consent, Philip and Anne Dacre were married. The following year, in 1572, the year of his father's execution, Philip went up to Cambridge and was awarded his degree in November 1576. Not long afterwards he was introduced to the magnificent court of Queen Elizabeth I. Philip had already acquired a taste for the good things of life at Cambridge and, dazzled by the allurements of the Court, he lived an extravagant life and soon became a favourite of the Queen (to whom he was related through the Queen's mother, Anne Boleyn, who was a Howard). In doing so he deserted his young wife, whom he left neglected and unhappy.

Conversion and Arrest

OPPOSITE:
The Long Gallery of Arundel Castle, now the library, where Philip made the fateful resolve to be reconciled to the Catholic faith.

On 24 February 1580, Philip's maternal grandfather, Henry Fitzalan, 12th Earl of Arundel, and the last of his line, died. Philip succeeded to the title and became the 13th Earl of Arundel, the premier earl of England. Philip, still only twenty-three years old, now took his place in the House of Lords and as he took a greater interest in the affairs of state so he spent less time at court.

His wife, Anne, had been baptized and brought up a Catholic but had subsequently conformed, at least outwardly, to the Elizabethan church. She now felt increasingly drawn to the faith of her baptism but quite apart from the risk of persecution, which was fierce at the time, she feared that she might now be placing a calamitous strain on her relations with Philip.

Nevertheless a priest was secretly brought into the castle at Arundel where Anne was reconciled to the Catholic Church. However to her astonishment Philip did not take offence at her reconciliation for, unknown to herself, he was already persuaded of the truth of the religion into which he, too, had been baptized. Philip had been unable to escape this conviction from the day he had attended the debate in the Tower of London between some protestant divines and the Jesuit priest, Edmund Campion, at which he was profoundly moved by the manifest sincerity and holiness of Campion 'that shone like a blinding light exposing the smart invective of his opponents'. This was the first decisive stage in Philip's reconciliation to the Catholic Church.

Some two years later Philip's wife, Anne, was expecting their first child. As a recusant (who refused to attend Church of England services) the Queen placed her under house arrest in the custody of Sir Thomas Shirley at his house in Wiston in Sussex; there she gave birth to her child, a daughter. Anxious to retain the Queen's favour at least for the time being, Philip had the child christened Elizabeth in the Protestant Church.

In 1584 Philip returned to the faith of his baptism. Tradition has it that it was in the Long Gallery of Arundel Castle (now the library) where his long mental struggle was finally resolved. Philip returned to Howard House in London where he was received into the Catholic Church by Fr. William Weston, the only Jesuit then at liberty in England.

This was no token conversion but a complete change of life for Philip. Philip kept a priest at Howard House, where his presence could be more easily concealed, from whom he could receive the sacraments frequently; prayer now became a regular part of his life. He continued to attend the Court and the House of Lords but avoided attending services on various pretexts.

However it was only a matter of time before his reconciliation became known. Philip's dilemma was how best to serve the Catholic cause. He wrote to Cardinal Allen in Douai (in Flanders, Northern France), the leader of the Catholic community in exile, but it appears that the letter was intercepted by agents of Sir Francis Walsingham, the Secretary of State and the Queen's spymaster, and a fictitious reply delivered advising him to fly to the continent. Fr. Weston had urged Philip to remain in England but he yielded to the apparent advice of Cardinal Allen.

Arrangements were made for Philip's departure and, saying goodbye to Anne who was now expecting their second child, Philip set sail from Littlehampton. Once into the open sea his ship was intercepted by a small warship commanded by Francis Kelloway who had been authorized by Walsingham to arrest the Earl and bring him back to London. On 25 April 1585 Philip was taken to the Tower of London where he was destined to spend almost the last 11 years of his life.

RIGHT:
A stained glass window in the Barons' Hall of Arundel Castle depicting Philip at the moment of decision: the figures in the background foreshadow his subsequent betrayal.

6

ST EDMUND CAMPION (1540–81)

Edmund Campion was educated at St John's College, Oxford, and ordained deacon in the Church of England in 1569. But in 1573 he entered the Jesuit Order and was ordained in 1578. In 1580 he joined the first Jesuit mission to England preaching extensively and with considerable effect in London and Lancashire. In the following year he secretly published a pamphlet: *Decem Rationes*, defending the Catholic Faith, which caused a considerable stir at Oxford.

In July 1581 Campion was imprisoned in the Tower of London where, after spending four days in the 'Little Ease', he was subjected to a number of interrogations on the rack. The Queen offered him liberty and honours if he would return to the Church of England, but he refused. Campion was a prize capture for the authorities and the Queen agreed to a request from the Court for a disputation between him and the Deans of Windsor and St Paul's. Campion, deprived of books and other aids and weakened by torture and scanty diet, was in stark contrast to his opponents who were armed with books, notes and prepared references.

In November 1581 Campion was charged with conspiracy against the Crown and condemned to death; he was hung, drawn and quartered on 1 December 1581.

Trial and Imprisonment

OPPOSITE:
Inscription engraved by Philip above the fireplace in his cell in the Beauchamp Tower; this is still clearly visible to visitors to the Tower today.

BELOW:
A stained glass window (also in the Barons' Hall of Arundel Castle) depicting Philip's resolve to remain steadfast in his faith; he is shown making his celebrated inscription on the wall of his cell.

RIGHT:
An engraving showing a Catholic being tortured for his faith.

RIGHT & OPPOSITE:
The Traitors' Gate of the Tower of London, the landing place for prisoners brought after trial for imprisonment and execution. Philip would have followed his cousins, Anne Boleyn and Catherine Howard, through these gates of no return.

After 12 months Philip appeared before the Court of Star Chamber on 15 May 1586. There were three principal charges: that he had attempted to leave the realm without the Queen's permission; that he had been reconciled to the Church of Rome; that he was plotting with foreign powers to be restored as Duke of Norfolk (this latter charge was later dropped). Philip was found guilty but, as treason was not alleged, he was fined £10,000 and imprisoned during the 'Queen's Pleasure'.

For the first two years of his imprisonment he was kept in solitary confinement in the Beauchamp Tower. His greatest trial was separation from his wife, Anne. Several times he wrote to the Queen seeking permission for Anne to visit him; not only was this refused but the news of the birth of his second child, a son, was withheld from him.

Subsequently Philip's conditions of imprisonment were eased, possibly because after the execution of Mary, Queen of Scots, he was perceived as less of a threat. He was enabled to make contact with other Catholic prisoners in the Tower, including Fr. William Bennett, a priest who occasionally celebrated mass in his cell with requisites smuggled in.

It was during this time that Philip carved the most famous of the three inscriptions on the walls of his cell (inscriptions that can be seen by visitors to the Tower today). Written in Latin it reads: *Quanto plus afflictionis pro Christo in hoc saeculo, tanto plus gloriae cum Christo in futuro.* 'The more suffering in this world for Christ's sake, the more glory with Christ in the next.' The high esteem in which Philip was held at the time by his fellow Catholics can be seen in the addition to this inscription by the next prisoner to occupy Philip's cell, a Catholic priest, Fr. Antony Tuchier, who added the words in Latin: *Gloria et honore coronasti eum domine* (with glory and honour you have crowned him, Lord. Ps 8:6) and: *In memoria aeterna erit justus* (the just will be held in everlasting remembrance).

ST ROBERT SOUTHWELL (1561–95)

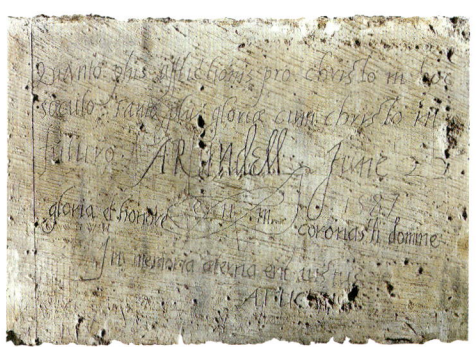

'Quanto plus afflictionis pro Christo
in hoc saeculo
Tanto plus gloriae cum Christo
in futuro'
ARUNDELL JUNE 22 1587

(The more affliction [we endure]
for Christ in this world,
The more glory [we shall obtain]
with Christ in the world to come.)

During his long years in the Tower, Philip received spiritual guidance and encouragement from Fr. Robert Southwell who in 1584, at the age of 23, had been ordained as a Jesuit priest in Rome.

He returned to England in 1586 as part of the Jesuit mission to the Catholics, one year after Philip's imprisonment in the Tower, and became chaplain to Philip's wife, Anne, at Arundel House in the Strand. Southwell was an accomplished writer and his letters to Philip during his long periods of imprisonment did much to strengthen his resolve. These were later published in the form of a book: *An Epistle of Comfort*.

Southwell was also a gifted organiser, responsible for getting candidates for the priesthood out of the country for training abroad and for finding secure accommodation for them on their return. Known by the authorities as 'the chief dealer for papists in England' he was ardently sought after by the infamous priest-hunter, Richard Topcliffe.

In 1592 Southwell was betrayed into the hands of Topcliffe who tortured him severely ten times over a period of four days but Southwell refused to disclose any names. He was transferred to the Tower and in February 1595 he was tried for treason on the grounds that he was a priest remaining in the country against the law of 1585 and condemned to be hung, drawn and quartered at Tyburn; the sentence was carried out immediately.

Although Philip and Robert Southwell never met, they nevertheless formed a strong friendship bonded by their common plight and determined faith. On one occasion Philip's dog visited Southwell in his cell; this was the closest contact they made and Philip said that he loved the dog the better for it.

The Spanish Armada

ABOVE:
Charles, Lord Howard of Effingham, a cousin of Philip, Lord High Admiral of England, who commanded the fleet that defeated the Spanish Armada. Philip was wrongfully accused of praying for the success of the Armada.

For much of the 16th century England and Spain were allies, not enemies. The Spanish Catherine of Aragon had married Henry VIII and their daughter, Mary, had married King Philip of Spain. After Mary's death, Philip had even made a proposal to Elizabeth I in the belief that influence over England was the key to successful defence against French supremacy in the Netherlands and might effect England's return to the Catholic faith.

England's relationship with Spain was only a small piece in the wider jigsaw of European politics where economic, strategic and religious rivalries created a complex web of ever-shifting alliances and international tensions. English support for the uprising in Philip's most troublesome province, the Netherlands, and the piratical campaigns against Spain's New World shipping – notably by Francis Drake – convinced Philip of the need to invade England. The Armada set sail in 1588.

The country was on full alert at the approach of this formidable force and rumours were current that a general massacre of Catholics sympathetic to the Catholic invader might ensue. Philip and some of his fellow prisoners prayed a 24-hour vigil for the safety of Catholics. At his trial in the following year Philip was to be charged (incorrectly) with praying for the success of the Armada.

In April 1589 Philip was put on trial for treason, the principal charges being that he had adopted Catholicism and attempted to leave the country without permission and that he had offered prayers and a mass for the success of the Spanish Armada. This Philip denied, declaring that he had offered prayers for the safety of Catholics during the crisis. The case against Philip on the second charge was flimsy to say the least but, to the dismay and sadness of the crowd awaiting the verdict, Philip was found guilty and condemned to death. This was perhaps the only

RIGHT:
The Armada Portrait of Queen Elizabeth I; the defeat of the Armada consolidated the Reformation in England and established the naval power that was to be a major influence in English history in the years ahead.

10

CONDEMNATION AND DEATH

case in English legal history where someone has been condemned as a traitor for prayer.

Such was the general revulsion against the Earl's condemnation that Elizabeth did not sign his death-warrant, but he was not informed of this decision. For six more years he lingered in the Tower under constant threat of death.

Shortly before his death, Philip petitioned the Queen for permission to see his wife and his son whom he had never seen. The Queen replied that if Philip would but once go to the Protestant church service, not only would she grant his request, but he should be restored to his estates and honours with as much favour as she could show. With great sorrow Philip replied that he could not accept the Queen's offer on such conditions.

Time took its toll and after Philip had spent almost 11 years in the Tower, he died on 19 October 1595. There were some suspicions that he may have been poisoned but there is no real evidence to sustain this. More likely the harsh conditions of prison life had produced their inevitable outcome. His body was laid in his father's grave in the chapel of St Peter ad Vincula in the Tower where it remained until 1624 when it was taken to a vault built for the family in Arundel.

> Not a bell sounded, but it might be his knell; not a footstep was heard, but it might be the messenger of death. Each morning, as he rose, he knew not but that, before night, he might be a headless corpse; each night, as he lay his head upon his pillow, he was uncertain whether the morning might not summon him to another world.

BELOW:
An engraving by Wenceslas Hollar in 1644 of the town and castle of Arundel. Note the river running in front of the town, down which Philip probably made his attempted escape to Europe.

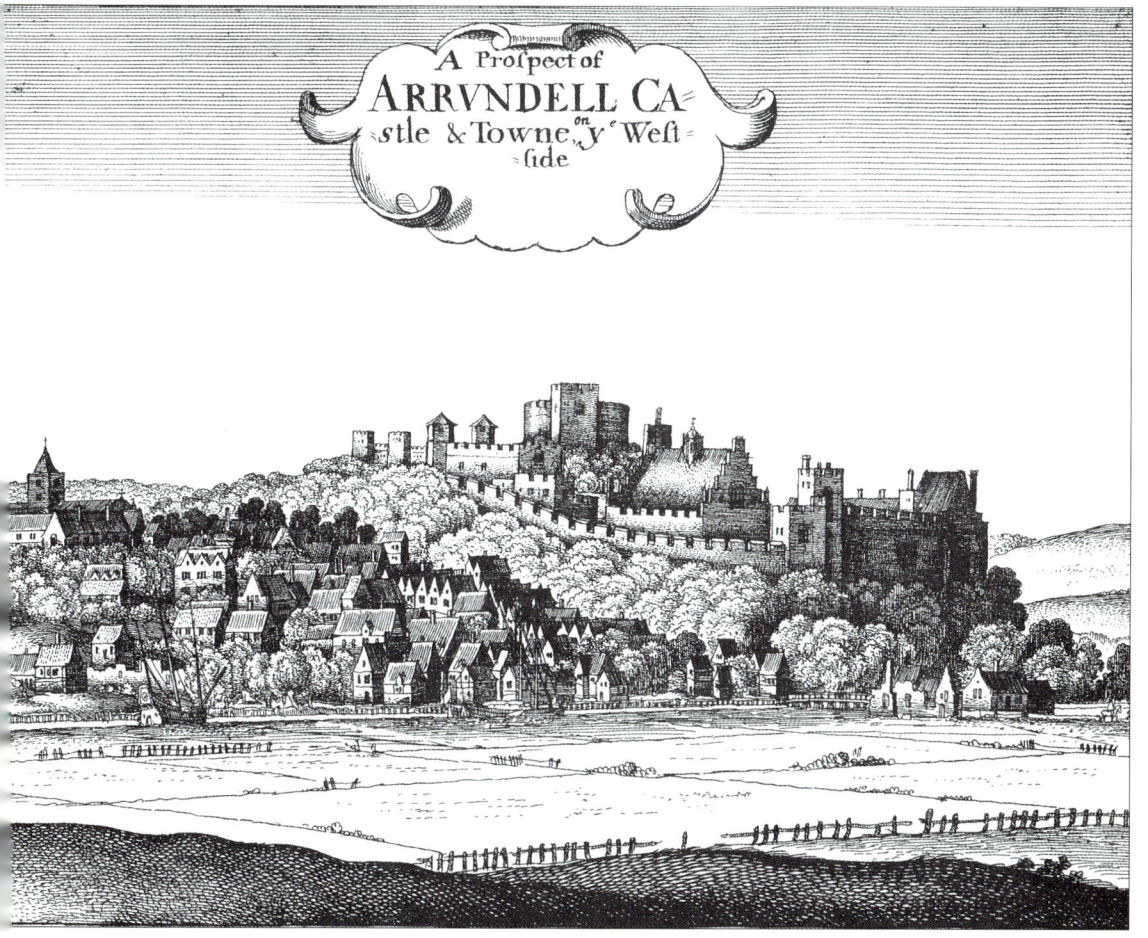

11

Canonization

BELOW:
Some of the Forty Martyrs of England and Wales, depicted celebrating the mass for which they died. Philip is on the right with his dog; Edmund Campion is immediately behind Margaret Ward (kneeling).

As the years went by conditions for Catholics gradually got easier but the memory of those who fought so ardently for the faith remained. In 1929 Philip was beatified (the first stage on the step to sainthood) by Pope Pius XI with others who had stood firm in the face of persecution and in October 1970 he was canonized by Pope Paul VI as one of the Forty Martyrs of England and Wales. Included in this number were Edmund Campion, whose defence of the faith set Philip on the course to reconciliation with the Catholic Church, and Robert Southwell, who had sustained Philip with his prayer and encouragement during his long years in the Tower.

In 1971 the remains of St Philip were brought from the Fitzalan Chapel (the burial chapel of the Fitzalan–Howard family) and enshrined in Arundel Cathedral. In 1973 the dedication of the Cathedral was changed from: 'Our Lady and St Philip Neri' to: 'Our Lady and St Philip Howard' and St Philip Howard became the patron saint of the diocese of Arundel and Brighton.

Devotion to St Philip has spread well beyond Surrey and Sussex to as far away as America and the Southern Hemisphere.